NEW BELIEVER'S CRASH COURSE

WORKBOOK

New Believer's Bible Study Guide Series

THOMAS A. LENZ

VAN VUUREN HOUSE

PUBLISHED BY:
VAN VUUREN HOUSE
Copyright © 2014
Edition 1.1

thomas.a.lenz@NewBelieversBibleStudyGuide.com

Except where noted, all Bible quotes from New King James Version.

INTRODUCTION

This book is written to "new believers." That is, to anyone who has just become a believer in Jesus Christ. If that describes you, congratulations, you've made the greatest decision of your life. You've been transformed from one type of being into another. You've stepped through The Door, Jesus, into a realm so vast that it will take you eternity to explore. This book is about helping you to understand what has happened to you and how to begin to fully realize all that now belongs to you.

Later in the book, I'll describe a little bit more about what happened to you when you became a believer. It is the most miraculous and significant event that can happen to a human being, and yet here's a fact that's both tragic and puzzling: not everyone, in fact most people, don't continue on to fulfill the destiny that God has provided for them. Jesus spoke of it this way:

> *Enter by the narrow gate; for wide is the gate and broad is the way that leads to destruction, and there are many who go in by it. Because narrow is the gate and difficult is the way which leads to life, and there are few who find it.* (Matthew 7:13)

How can this be? If God's gift to mankind through Jesus is so wonderful and so magnificent, why is the whole world not immediately and whole-heartedly rushing to accept it and falling at the feet of Jesus in thanksgiving and adoration? Part of the answer is in the verse just quoted. The many who are on the path to destruction exert a strong influence on those around them that pulls in the same direction that they are going, to destruction. Have you ever tried to enter a door into a building that everyone else was leaving? It can be quite a challenge to go against the flow.

Another part of the answer is that a believer has some enemies. Who are these enemies? What are their tactics? How can their tactics be defeated? These are some of the things that you will learn in the New Believer's Crash Course.

I've been a believer for over four decades. I know what has helped me be victorious over the strategies of our enemies. I've seen many casualties and the tactics to which they fell victim. I've also seen how others have stayed strong and have made great progress toward the prize to which God in Christ is calling us. As I have observed all these things, I've made mental notes: "Here is a trap, don't fall for it." "Here is an overcoming strategy, do this." I've asked myself, "What if I only had one chance to tell someone what they need to know to be one of those few who find, and stay on, the way that leads to life? My answer to that question is the New Believer's Crash Course. I've endeavored to make it as short, yet as complete as possible. I am confident that if you will apply these truths seriously and diligently, on the day that you stand before the Lord and give account for what you did in this life you will hear "Well done, you good and faithful servant, enter in to the joy of your Lord."

CONTENTS

CHAPTER 1
WHAT JUST HAPPENED TO ME?

So you're a believer. How did you become a believer? Somebody told you about Jesus, or perhaps you read about Him, and you believed the message and responded to it. You are now "saved." Becoming a believer saves you from sin, sickness and spiritual death. Spiritual death means separation from God. If your body had died while you were spiritually dead, you would have spent eternity in hell. (See what I mean about having made the greatest decision of your life?)

Romans 10:8-13 spells out how that works:

> *But what does it say? "The word is near you, in your mouth and in your heart" (that is, the word of faith which we preach): that if you confess with your mouth the Lord Jesus and believe in your heart that God has raised Him from the dead, you will be saved. For with the heart one believes unto righteousness, and with the mouth confession is made unto salvation. For the Scripture says, "Whoever believes on Him will not be put to shame." For there is no distinction between Jew and Greek, for the same Lord over all is rich to all who call upon Him. For "whoever calls on the name of the Lord shall be saved."*

You are saved when you believe what the Bible says about Jesus, and you express this from your heart with your mouth. What you say exactly is not important, and what you experience at the time is not important. What you believe is the important part.

For example, I was raised Catholic. We were taught to pray the Apostle's Creed:

I believe in God, the Father Almighty,
    the Maker of heaven and earth,
    and in Jesus Christ, His only Son, our Lord:

Who was conceived by the Holy Ghost,
    born of the virgin Mary,
    suffered under Pontius Pilate,
    was crucified, dead, and buried;

He descended into hell.
The third day He arose again from the dead;
He ascended into heaven,
    and sitteth on the right hand of God the Father Almighty;
    from thence he shall come to judge the quick and the dead.
I believe in the Holy Ghost;
    the holy catholic church;
    the communion of saints;

the forgiveness of sins;
the resurrection of the body;
and the life everlasting.
 Amen.

 This prayer expresses well what Romans 10:9 tells us to believe to be saved. However, as a Catholic, I must have said this prayer hundreds of times without anything at all happening. Saying a prayer is different than actually praying. I mentally assented to the words of the prayer, but I had no idea that God might actually respond to my prayer. I was merely reciting from memory. Then one day someone showed me Romans 10:8-13. This scripture made me realize that if I prayed that same prayer, believing God would do something, He would - I would be saved. So I prayed something like the Apostle's Creed once more, this time believing that God would save me, and that's when my life with God began. The action was the same, but the believing was different. Believing made the difference.

1. What made you decide to become a believer?

   _____

   _____

2. What is it like to be a believer?

   _____

   _____

3. Why do you think there are not more believers in the world?

   _____

   _____

4. What kinds of things could cause you to turn away from God?

   _____

   _____

5. If you are a believer, you are saved. What are you saved from?

   _____

   _____

6. Who would you like to tell about Jesus?

   _____

   _____

It would be hard to overstate the role that faith plays in a believer's life. In fact, 'believer' means someone who lives by faith. (To believe and to have faith are synonymous terms. They come from the same root Greek word.)

John 3:16-18:

For God so loved the world that He gave His only begotten Son, that whoever believes in Him should not perish but have everlasting life. For God did not send His Son into the world to condemn the world, but that the world through Him might be saved. He who believes in Him is not condemned; but he who does not believe is condemned already, because he has not believed in the name of the only begotten Son of God.

God gave His only Son. Who receives that gift? *"Whoever believes in Him."* The thing that decides whether a person has eternal life is faith, faith in Jesus Christ. Imagine a line of all the people who have ever lived standing one behind another single file, sorted according to the good and bad things they did in their lives, the most evil person on one end, and the most holy on the other end. Some people's idea of how God chooses who goes to heaven and who goes to hell is that He finds a place in that line and says "OK, this person is good enough to go to heaven. Everyone from here forward goes to heaven, and the rest of you go to hell." No! Faith, or believing, is what determines your eternal destination. Quoting again from John 3:18, *"He who believes in Him is not condemned; but he who does not believe is condemned"*

It's important to note here that eternal life refers not only to length of life, but the quality of life as well. In the seventeenth chapter of the same book, Jesus defines eternal life as knowing God and knowing Jesus. Now here is a simple truth, the full light of which has not dawned on most people: eternal life begins the moment you are saved. People make a huge mistake when they think that so much of what the Bible promises only comes into effect after a person dies physically.

In the last chapter of Mark, Jesus said:

"Go into all the world and preach the gospel to every creature. "He who believes and is baptized will be saved; but he who does not believe will be condemned. (Mark 16:15-16)

Faith is what separates the saved from the condemned!

Actually, Jesus paid the price for the sins of every person who was ever born or will ever be born, but it will not benefit anyone until they believe.

If you think about it for a moment, this is radically different from what religion teaches. Religion teaches us that we have to be really good so that God can accept us. That we have to earn right standing with God. When we are so good that God accepts us, we deserve congratulations from God. In contrast, the Bible teaches us that no person can be good enough to gain right standing with God. The only way to be right is to accept it as the gift that Jesus paid for. We could put it this way:

Religion says "I do the work, God accepts my work, and I get the glory."

The Bible says "God did the work, I accept His work, He gets the glory."

To summarize what got set in motion when you became a believer: God did a number of things in you and for you the instant that you became a believer, and there are a number of things that He will do in you and for you as you live the life that He has destined for you. Put another way, a seed was planted in you, now you have to care for that seed so that it will grow. Put yet another way, now that God has done a great work in you, there is some work for you to do. Not work in the sense that you have to do things to earn acceptance or salvation from God, but work in the sense that there are some things you have to do in order to reap the benefits of what God has already done for you.

For example, if I told you that in a certain place on my property there is buried treasure and you can have all of it that you find, you would have to do some things to get the treasure into your hands. First of all, you would have to believe what I told you about its existence and location. If you didn't believe me you would just ignore what I said and do without. Believing me would lead you to get a shovel or something to dig with, and you would then have to dig until you found the treasure. None of this work has to do with earning something from me or trying to convince me to give it to you, because I gave the treasure to you to start with. But the treasure won't do you any good until you expend some effort to dig it up and carry it away. In the same way, there are many things that God has given to you as a believer, but you will have to do your part before you can reap the benefit of them.

CHAPTER 2
WHAT SHOULD I DO NOW?

Although we are saved by believing, faith without corresponding action is dead. One of the actions that must accompany becoming a believer is repentance. To repent means to make a change for the better as a result of being sorry for your sins. Good works don't save us, but we are saved so that we can do good works. After all, we would question the sincerity of anyone who, on the one hand says he's a believer in Jesus, but on the other hand still intends to live as he did before he became a believer. The idea is to conform our lives to Jesus Christ, not to make Him conform to our lives.

The right reaction is modeled by Saul (who later became the apostle Paul) when he became a believer. He said "Lord, what do you want me to do?" (Acts 9:6) That's a question we should all constantly ask.

Let's look again at (Mark 16:15-16):

"Go into all the world and preach the gospel to every creature. "He who believes and is baptized will be saved; but he who does not believe will be condemned. (Mark 16:15-16)

It says "He who believes and is baptized will be saved." This verse is referring to water baptism. Although being water baptized is not what saves us, it is still one of the first things that a new believer should do. It gives action to and demonstrates his faith. It is an outward sign of an inner work. Peter had this to say about it in Acts 2:38:

Repent, and let every one of you be baptized in the name of Jesus Christ for the remission of sins; and you shall receive the gift of the Holy Spirit.

Here Peter exhorts people to repent and be baptized. He also mentions the gift of the Holy Spirit, which is actually the main subject of Peter's discourse in Acts 2. Getting baptized in the Holy Spirit is one of the gifts that God is anxious for new believers to receive. The apostles made getting new believers baptized in the Holy Spirit a top priority. You can find out more about it in my book "How Can I Get the Holy Spirit Today". See details at www. newbelieversbiblestudyguide.com.

One of the main things that happens to a person when he is saved is that he is born again.

Jesus speaks of this in John's gospel:

There was a man of the Pharisees named Nicodemus, a ruler of the Jews. This man came to Jesus by night and said to Him, "Rabbi, we know that You are a teacher come from God; for no one can do these signs that You do unless God is with him." Jesus answered and said to him, "Most assuredly, I say to you, unless one is born again, he cannot see the kingdom of God." Nicodemus said to Him, "How can a man be born when he is old? Can he enter a second time into his mother's womb and be born?" Jesus answered, "Most assuredly, I say to you, unless one is born of water and the Spirit, he cannot enter the kingdom of God. "That which is born of the flesh is flesh, and that which is born of the Spirit is spirit. "Do not marvel that I said to you, 'You must be born again.' (John 3:1-7)

To understand what Jesus is talking about here, it's important to understand something about what kind of creatures human beings are. We are spirit, we have a soul, and we live in a body. The spirit, or heart as the Bible sometimes calls it, is who we are, it's the eternal part of us. The soul is the part of us associated with our mind. The soul is the source of our will, our thoughts, our likes and dislikes, and our emotions. The soul is the part of us that senses emotion.

When Jesus spoke about being born again, Nicodemus took it to mean that He was talking about being physically born again. But Jesus explained that yes, you have to be physically born, born of water, born of the flesh, to even be eligible to be born of the spirit. To enter the kingdom of God, you must also be born of the spirit. Physical birth gains you access into the earth, spiritual birth gains you access into the kingdom of God.

The reason a person needs to be born again is that because of sin, he is spiritually dead, separated from God. To sin means to do something that you know is wrong. Everyone has done something that they know is wrong, everyone has sinned. Sin separates us from God. A being that has become corrupted by sin cannot be united with God, but God wants us to be united with Him. When we are born again, our old selves actually die, and we are born again as entirely new creatures.

> *Therefore, if anyone is in Christ, he is a new creation; old things have passed away; behold, all things have become new.* (2 Corinthians 5:17)

According to Strong's Lexicon of Greek words, 'new' in this verse can mean 'a new kind.' You are born again as a new kind of being. This is the real you, your spirit, that this verse is talking about. Outwardly or physically, there is not necessarily a change in appearance. Sometimes people's bodies will get healed or their countenance will become more peaceful or joyful, but these are side effects of the new birth. The spirit is recreated and given the nature of God.

In Romans, we can read some more detail about the new birth:

> *We know that our old (unrenewed) self was nailed to the cross with Him in order that [our] body [which is the instrument] of sin might be made ineffective and inactive for evil, that we might no longer be the slaves of sin. For when a man dies, he is freed (loosed, delivered) from [the power of] sin [among men]. Now if we have died with Christ, we believe that we shall also live with Him, Because we know that Christ (the Anointed One), being once raised from the dead, will never die again; death no longer has power over Him. For by the death He died, He died to sin [ending His relation to it] once for all; and the life that He lives, He is living to God [in unbroken fellowship with Him]. Even so consider yourselves also dead to sin and your relation to it broken, but alive to God [living in unbroken fellowship with Him] in Christ Jesus.* (Romans 6:6-11 AMP)

Review Questions

1. What did you have to do to earn salvation?

    _____

    _____

2. What causes a person to be condemned to hell?

    _____

    _____

3. What does it mean to repent?

    _____

    _____

4. What things in your life do you need to repent of?

    _____

    _____

5. What does it mean to be born again?

    _____

    _____

6. Are spiritual things less real because they are unseen?

    _____

Sin no longer has power over you! Some people don't see that as a good thing, they want to sin. That's part of the power sin has. The power over you that caused you to desire to sin is now broken! You are now remade in the image of Jesus, of whom God said "You have loved righteousness and hated lawlessness." (Hebrews 1:9) You may not feel like that now. That's OK, believe it. You are now walking by faith and not by sight. That means that what you believe is more important than what you see. ('See' here means sense with your physical senses or understand with your natural mind.) As you go forward believing, you will begin to see what you believe. Your tastes will change. What you used to love, you'll begin to hate. What you used to hate you'll begin to love. You'll look back and thank God for rescuing you from being such a fool as to love some of the things that you now hate.

Much of what is written in the letters in the New Testament describes who we are and what belongs to us as new creatures. For example, Romans 5:1 says:

> *"Therefore, having been justified by faith, we have peace with God through our Lord Jesus Christ,"*

Justified means that God sees you as perfectly innocent. You can remember what "justified" means this way: "It's just as if I'd never sinned." Because of the precious blood of Jesus that was shed for you, you are completely washed of any sin that you have ever done. The Bible says that God forgets your sin!

> *"I, even I, am He who blots out your transgressions for My own sake;*
> *And I will not remember your sins.* (Isaiah 43:25)

God forgot your sins, now so must you. Savor how great it is to live in peace with God!

I'll list here some main differences between old creatures and new creatures:

Old creatures:
Are children of the devil (John 8:44)
Live under the power of darkness (Col 1:13)
Are darkness (2 Cor 6:14)
Are lawless (2 Cor 6:14)
Are temples of idols (2 Cor 6:14)
Are slaves of sin (Romans 6:17)
Are strangers of the covenants of promise (Ephesians 2:12)
Have no hope (Ephesians 2:12)
Are without God (Ephesians 2:12)
Headed for hell (Ephesians 2:3)

New creatures:
Are children of God (1 John 3:1)
Live in the kingdom of God (Col 1:13)

14

Are light (2 Cor 6:14)
Are righteous (2 Cor 6:14)
Are temples of God (2 Cor 6:14)
Are obedient (Romans 6:17)
Have been brought near (Ephesians 2:12)
Are begotten again to a living hope (1 Peter 1:3)
Are one with God (John 17:21)
Remain with God forever (Revelation 22:5)

Now you can see that no matter how spectacular of an experience people have at the moment that they are born again, it cannot begin to compare with what in reality happens to them.

> *The kingdom of heaven is like a mustard seed, which a man took and sowed in his field, which indeed is the least of all the seeds; but when it is grown it is greater than the herbs and becomes a tree, so that the birds of the air come and nest in its branches.* (Matthew 13:31-32)

The beginning of a mustard seed tree's life is not at all spectacular. A small seed buried in the ground remains unseen for a number of days. Then, a tiny leaf appears. Slowly, slowly, it grows bigger and stronger. Just so, when you made the decision to proclaim your faith in Jesus, it may have seemed like a small gesture. Maybe you didn't notice any big change in your life right away. Different people have different experiences. As I already mentioned, the magnitude and type of experience makes no eternal difference at all. What matters now is that you continue to water that seed.

> *having been born again, not of corruptible seed but incorruptible, through the word of God which lives and abides forever, because "All flesh is as grass, And all the glory of man as the flower of the grass. The grass withers, And its flower falls away, But the word of the Lord endures forever." Now this is the word which by the gospel was preached to you.* (1 Peter 1:22-25)

CHAPTER 3

FLOURISHING

Now that the incorruptible seed is planted in you, how should you care for it?

If you've spent some time taking care of plants, you know that if you give them the kind of fertilizer, watering and environment they like, it makes a big difference. They'll have a healthy, dark green color. They will grow quickly, have lush foliage, and be stronger against diseases and pests. The same is true for the eternal seed in you. For healthy growth you need to consistently do these six things:

1. Feed on the Word of God.
2. Talk to God and expect Him to talk to you.
3. Be obedient to what God tells you.
4. Worship God
5. Fellowship with other believers
6. Tell other people about Jesus.

1. FEED ON THE WORD OF GOD

Get in the habit of taking some time each day to read the Bible. At this point, consistency is better than quantity. 15 minutes every day is better than 2 hours once a week. Personally, I find that consistency in terms of time of day and place is also helpful. I like to read sitting in the armchair in our living room, right when I wake up. Having said that, it's also good to take a Bible snack at random times. Sometimes you'll get quite a lot out of taking a moment to read even just one verse.

Don't worry if you don't understand everything you read. For the most part, it's good not to get stuck trying to figure out everything you read. Just read on and God will eventually make clear to you the meaning.

Start reading the Bible in the New Testament. This is the part that applies to the time we now live in. The Letter of James and The Gospel According to John are good places to start. In the Old Testament, Proverbs and Psalms are readily understandable.

There are different ways to read. Sometimes it's good to read large portions. Sometimes it's good to take a lot of time looking at one verse. Sometimes it's good to research a certain subject.

You will find that you will start to develop a deep love of God's word. You'll say with the psalmist *"I rejoice at Your word as one who finds great treasure."* (Psalm 119:162)

Throughout history, God has chosen to reveal Himself to us, not by what He looks like or by anything else that we can sense with our five senses, but by what He says. Jesus quotes the Old Testament in Matthew 4:4:

"Man shall not live by bread alone, but by every word that proceeds from the mouth of God. " (Matthew 4:4)

That's why what God speaks is called the Word of Life. It's absolutely vital to our life and well being. Everything we know was created by God's word and all things are held together by His word. The first chapter of John's Gospel says that there is not one thing that has come into existence apart from the word of God.

as newborn babes, desire the pure milk of the word, that you may grow thereby, (1 Peter 2:2)

Newborn babes get desperate for milk. It's almost as if they're in intense pain when it's time for them to eat, and when they finally get to drink, the milk is like a soothing potion for them. Let yourself be as desperate to hear from God through His word as newborn babes are for milk.

I'll explain a little bit about what the word of God does for us.

As I mentioned before, as humans, we are spirit, we live in a body and we have a soul. Here is a scripture that illustrates that fact:

Now may the God of peace Himself sanctify you completely; and may your whole spirit, soul, and body be preserved blameless at the coming of our Lord Jesus Christ. (1 Thessalonians 5:23)

We've noted previously that when a person is born again, it is the spirit part of them that is immediately affected. However, the soul is not saved instantly, but through a process. The Holy Spirit through James said:

Therefore lay aside all filthiness and overflow of wickedness, and receive with meekness the implanted word, which is able to save your souls. (James 1:21)

As a person receives the word and is a doer of it, the soul is molded into the image of Christ. Romans 12:2 says something similar:

And do not be conformed to this world, but be transformed by the renewing of your mind, that you may prove what is that good and acceptable and perfect will of God.

Practically speaking, what does this look like? In general, before people are born again they have sinful habits, ungodly character traits, and unholy desires. These don't change the moment they are saved. But as their minds are renewed, people begin to change bad habits for good habits. They learn to walk in love and live in a joyful and peaceful state of mind regardless of circumstances. Hunger for God and His word replace the desire for unholy things.

1. How much time could you spend each day reading your Bible? (Choose an amount of time that you are at least 90% certain that you will spend every day.)

    _____

    _____

2. Is the type of experience a person has when he or she gets saved important?

    _____

    _____

3. What's the relationship between spirit, soul and body?

    _____

    _____

4. Why did Jesus say that we live by every word that comes from the mouth of God?

    _____

    _____

5. How does God create things?

    _____

    _____

6. Are there any particular scriptures that stand out to you now?

    _____

    _____

2. TALK TO GOD AND EXPECT HIM TO TALK TO YOU.

Take time each day to fellowship with God. Thank Him for what He has done and is doing for you. Maintaining a thankful attitude will keep you strong. Ask Him for guidance. Expect Him to make the answer clear to you. Most of the time, people don't hear God speak with their natural ears. Most often, God will guide you with your conscience. A knowing will come to you. For example, clearly you heard from God when you decided to accept Jesus. How did that come to you? That was God leading you.

"My sheep hear My voice, and I know them, and they follow Me." (John 10:27)

Also, you can expect God to speak to you through His written word. While you're reading the Bible, sometimes a certain scripture will seem to resonate with you. This is God speaking to you by emphasizing that scripture. God will speak to you through other believers. God also speaks through ministers – apostles, prophets, evangelists, pastors and teachers.

It is a mistake to expect God to guide you by circumstances. Jesus said that it's the Holy Spirit who guides us into all truth and teaches us all things. (John 16:13, 14:26) For example, I once heard someone say "I lost my car keys. That means God is telling me…" I forget what God was supposed to be telling him, but this is wrong. God doesn't steal your car keys or make you sick or anything else like that to teach you. He teaches you by the Holy Spirit.

God doesn't teach us by circumstances because, contrary to popular opinion, God is not in control of everything. God gave every person a free will and dominion over the earth. What He gives, He doesn't take back. People commit crimes and do unethical things exactly opposite of God's will all the time. Plus, because of Adam's sin, the whole earth is in bondage to corruption. Jesus told us to pray that God's will be done on earth as it is in heaven. (Matthew 6:10) So, instead of seeing what happens and saying "Oh, that was God's will," we look in the Bible and listen to the Holy Spirit to find God's will and then we cause it to happen by praying for it.

There's a lot we could say about discerning the voice of God, but for a start, you'll find it helpful to keep this simple bit of theology in mind:

God is good. The devil is bad. God doesn't do bad things to you. The devil does bad things, then blames God for them.

3. BE OBEDIENT TO WHAT GOD TELLS YOU

As you come to know the truth more fully, you will find that much more of your life is determined by the choices that you make than you realized. People blame God, the devil, circumstances, chance and so on, for things that were actually caused by their own decisions. Decisions determine direction, direction determines destiny.

I call heaven and earth as witnesses today against you, that I have set before you life and death, blessing and cursing; therefore choose life, that both you and your descendants may live; (Deuteronomy 30:19)

Choosing to obey God is choosing life. Temptations to disobey God come in all kinds of ways. For example, for most people it will almost always seem that there's not enough time for reading the Bible, praying, attending church, etc. Choose to do it anyway. God may tell you to sever a relationship. It may be very painful, but choose to obey God and you will find life in it.

Frequently new believers find that they have to change the music they listen to. Consider the lyrics of what you're hearing. Is it doing you any good to listen to that kind of thing? You will find that some music, even apart from the words, will make you fill icky on the inside. That means that the music is bringing death. Choose life. Decide right now to choose life in all things.

God does not require a complete change overnight, but He will begin to show you things that He wants you to change. Decide now, that as He shows you what to do and how to do it, that you will obey Him. Decide to simply follow Jesus. Do what He shows you to do. It will make for you a simple and beautiful life.

Here is an example that shows how we can change in God's strength and not our own. I know a woman who used to smoke cigarettes. She knew it wasn't pleasing to the Lord. One day she told her husband, "I am just going to forget about smoking cigarettes." So, rather than exercising her will power to resist the habit, she believed that God would cause her to forget about smoking. Soon after she spoke this to her husband, she realized that she had gone several days without smoking, simply because she forgot to. She got victory over the cigarette habit, not by trying hard, but by depending on God.

4. WORSHIP GOD

Part of talking to God should include worship. Lift your hands to Him and express your love to Him. Sing to Him. It can be a song that you make up as you go, or something that you remember. Both public and private worship should be a part of every believer's life.

5. FELLOWSHIP WITH OTHER BELIEVERS

If you are a new believer, one of the first things you'll have to do is get a new set of friends. This involves making new friends as well as separating yourself from your old friends. Godly friends can be a great source of strength and agents of change in your life. Old friends can hold you back, influencing you to keep your old ways and old habits.

In some cases, separating yourself from your old friends may be quite difficult, but it's absolutely necessary. Old friends can easily influence you to go back to old ways.

Do not be deceived: "Evil company corrupts good habits." (1 Corinthians 15:33)

He who walks with wise men will be wise, But the companion of fools will be destroyed. (Proverbs 13:20)

A new believer's natural reaction is to at once go and tell his old friends about Jesus. This is the right kind of desire to have, but in certain circumstances it's got many a new believer into trouble. It's wiser for a person to become well established in the Word and spiritually strong before he tries to win his friends.

Here's an example of the kind of situation a person should avoid: Let's say a fellow who used to be an alcoholic is newly born again, and has successfully stayed completely away from alcohol for a good while. He hears about some old friends of his that are all gathered at someone's house and he's invited. He thinks, "Oh this is a perfect chance to tell my old friends about Jesus." He arrives and finds his friends well drunk and still drinking. He does a great job of telling them about the joy he's found in Jesus, but they don't understand. They say "Ah come on, just one drink, you'll be fine." Next thing he knows is he wakes up somewhere and can't remember how he got there. A good rule of thumb about being around unbelievers is, as long as you're influencing them, it's fine. If they're influencing you, run!

One of the most important decisions you will ever make in your life is where you go to church. Ask God to help you find a good one and don't switch unless He tells you to. You will never have all that God has for you unless you become involved with a church. It's not just a matter of showing up at meetings a few times a week, but finding ways to contribute your time and resources.

You may hear the statement "I can be a Christian and not go to church." That's like saying "I can be married and still have a mistress." A married person with a mistress has broken the marriage covenant. There may be some outward signs of marriage, but the basic part of what marriage is intended to be is shredded. Likewise a Christian who wants to see himself as a Christian but has decided to be disobedient, is completely missing the heart of what it means to be a Christian.

You might find that there is not a single church where you live that has any life in it. Move to a locality that has a good church. If it means taking a job with lower pay, transplanting your family, moving away from relatives, leaving the comfort of the place you've called home, it's worth it. Now that may seem like a radical statement, but from an eternal perspective, it's merely reasonable good sense. Ten thousand years from now, what's going to be important? Whether you had a better job or that you put yourself in a position to receive God's best spiritual provision? Plus, it's just like God to take something that seems like a sacrifice and turn it into something that is a huge blessing in the here and now. For example that lower paying job may lead to an unexpectedly higher paying and more enjoyable one. Besides that, let's not forget that pursuing God's will benefits not only ourselves, but also our wives, our children, our grandchildren, friends, co-workers, acquaintances – everyone whose life we touch.

Again, the kingdom of heaven is like a merchant seeking beautiful pearls, who, when he had found one pearl of great price, went and sold all that he had and bought it. (Matthew 13:45-46)

For our light affliction, which is but for a moment, is working for us a far more exceeding and eternal weight of glory, while we do not look at the things which are seen, but at the things which are not seen. For the things which are seen are temporary, but the things which are not seen are eternal. (2 Corinthians 4:17-18)

For bodily exercise profits a little, but godliness is profitable for all things, having promise of the life that now is and of that which is to come. (1 Timothy 4:8)

Whatever sacrifice you have to make to be a part of a good church is well worth it, in this life and the one to come.

1. How does God communicate with you?

   _____

   _____

2. Would God make you sick or take some of your belongings to teach you something?

   _____

   _____

3. Can you identify past friendships that have helped or hurt you?

   _____

   _____

4. As you have read through this section and seen what God's word says about friendship, what changes have you decided to make concerning your friendships?

   _____

   _____

5. List your top 5 priorities in life from most important to least important.

   _____

   _____

6. TELL OTHER PEOPLE ABOUT JESUS.

Those who are wise shall shine
Like the brightness of the firmament,
And those who turn many to righteousness
Like the stars forever and ever. (Daniel 12:3)

Preach the word! Be ready in season and out of season. Convince, rebuke, exhort, with all longsuffering and teaching. (2 Timothy 4:2)

Then He said to them, "Follow Me, and I will make you fishers of men." (Matthew 4:19)

One of the few eternal things that we have contact with are people. All of those that you can influence to accept Jesus will be eternally grateful to you.

CHAPTER 4
WHAT TO DO IF YOU MAKE A MISTAKE

Jesus is the only one that has lived a perfect life. The rest of us make mistakes from time to time. What you do after you make the mistake is critical. When you find that you have sinned, make sure you:

1. Ask God to forgive you
2. Know that God forgives you
3. Forgive yourself
4. Decide not to repeat the mistake
5. Ask anyone you may have hurt to forgive you.

1. ASK GOD TO FORGIVE YOU

When you make a mistake, it's important for you to face up to what you did. Name the sin for what it is. Don't make excuses. Don't confess your sin wholesale, or in a general way, but in detail. Call each sin by its exact, ugly name. Confessing your sin this way will help you develop a hatred for it. Condemn your sin, not yourself. Separate yourself from it. You can say "I did that, but it is not me. It's something that I did."

You never want to be flippant about sin or asking God to forgive you. God hates sin and Jesus paid a horrible price for your sin. Allow yourself to be deeply sorry for your sin and mindful of the price that was paid for it.

2. KNOW THAT GOD FORGIVES YOU

> *If we confess our sins, He is faithful and just to forgive us our sins and to cleanse us from all unrighteousness. If we say that we have not sinned, we make Him a liar, and His word is not in us.*(1 John 1:9-10)

When we sin, our own hearts condemn us. Always remember, no matter what you have done, God is still on your side. He is not the one making you feel condemned about what you have done, it's your own heart. Jesus has already paid the price for your sin. Know that God forgives you and expect Him to cleanse you of the bad feeling that you have inside as a result of your actions. Jesus shed His blood so that we can be free from all the harmful effects of sin.

3. FORGIVE YOURSELF

Sometimes this is not easy. For one thing, even though God has forgiven you, you may still have to live with the bad results of what you did. Maybe you broke something in your anger. You ask God to forgive you and He does, but the thing is still broken. The tendency is to want to punish yourself. Don't do it.

Brethren, I do not count myself to have apprehended; but one thing I do, forgetting those things which are behind and reaching forward to those things which are ahead, (Philippians 3:13)

When you make a mistake, repent properly, then forget about it and look ahead.

Let's say for example that you got angry with someone right before church. You said some cruel things that made someone feel badly. Now you feel badly. But church starts and it's time to worship God. You feel like such a hypocrite. You think "Here I am, calling myself a Christian, but I'm a hypocrite. I haven't walked in love very well." You were a hypocrite all right. You were a hypocrite when you got angry and said some cruel things. You are a new creature and it's hypocritical for a new creature to act like the devil. But now that you are worshiping God you are not being hypocritical, you are now acting like who you really are. You are a new creature who loves to express love to God.

Here is a helpful, true story about repenting from Patsy Cameneti:

> Sometimes there is one area that you keep making the same mistake. The first time you say, Lord I'm sorry. Then when you come to the Lord, you think that he is not taking you seriously. So you say "I'm really sorry." The third time you come to him. "Now I'm really, really sorry."
>
> On one thing I was many reallys down the road. I stayed after work in my office. I was really sorry. I mostly was really sorry because of a fear that God would get grieved with me and the anointing would lift from off of my life and I would be stuck with the call and no anointing to do it. And then I would have to face Him without finishing my course.
>
> I was on my face in my office. I started weeping and wailing. I could not stand to feel like I grieved God. I said "I know what I'll do, I just won't talk to anybody the rest of the week, I'll just be real quiet. I'll just stay in this depressed state. I won't eat all week. I want God to know how sorry I am, I just won't eat. I'm just going to read my Bible. I may stay up half the night studying. I'll just stay by myself, just stay closed up to everyone. " God has not spoken to me sharply very many times. But He said, "Get up from there and stop that." Sometimes He speaks comfortingly to you. This wasn't one of those times. I stopped immediately.
>
> I sat there and was quiet for a little bit. And the Lord said, "Who do you think you are, that your sin is so special that my son's blood isn't quite good enough for you? That you have to do something extra because my son's sacrifice wasn't quite good enough for you? Who do you think you are that your sin was so special, that all of my infinite mercy wasn't quite good enough for you, that you have to add something to my son's work?" Then I was sorry for something else. I will never forget the tone of his voice.
>
> I would never consciously look at the cross and say "Well, Jesus, that was nice, but I need to do this too. I need to be depressed over this for a few days. I appreciate it, but I need to flog myself a little bit. I know the blood was shed but you know it wasn't just quite good enough."

That is so blasphemous, we would never do that, and yet by ignoring what He did and trying to go about establishing our own righteousness, it is a slap in his face.

So after he jerked the slack out of me, He said "Would you like to get back at the devil for tripping you up in this area? Get up and walk out of here like you never did a thing wrong!"

I could be bold because the blood of Jesus did the work.

4. DECIDE NOT TO REPEAT THE MISTAKE

As Jesus told a woman caught in adultery, "Neither do I condemn you; go and sin no more," so he tells us. If He commands you do to something, it means you can do it.

5. ASK ANYONE YOU MAY HAVE HURT TO FORGIVE YOU

Therefore if you bring your gift to the altar, and there remember that your brother has something against you, leave your gift there before the altar, and go your way. First be reconciled to your brother, and then come and offer your gift. (Matthew 5:23-24)

As always, following God's directions gives the best results. Here is an example from William A. Ward's book "The Miracles I Have Seen:"

Chapter 39 – The Deacon Who Would Not "Deak"

I was pastoring a church in Maryland, and I had a deacon that would not "deak." Now, if there is anything worse than a "non-deaking deacon," I don't know what it would be. The fellow declared, "As long as Brother Ward preaches in the church, I will never darken the door again." He had the church about split in half; half of the people thought that he was right and half thought the he was wrong. I was only nineteen, and I put the church absolutely first. Anything that hurt the church had to be wrong.

Two months went by, and his wife called me. She said, "I want you to come and pray for my husband; he is dying."

I answered, "Thank God!"

She remarked, "You misunderstood me; I said that he is dying."

I affirmed, "I did not misunderstand you; I have been praying for something to happen."

She continued, "Will you come and pray for him?" I averred, "I will come, but he has wronged the whole church, and I am not coming alone. I am not coming unless I can bring the whole church with me."

She cried, "Let me go ask him." She returned to the phone, shouting, "Bring them all!"

Now, let me digress to explain what had made him so angry. At a Sunday morning service, he told me that he owed God $400 back tithes and asked me what he should do. I told him that he should pay it. I continued, "If you don't pay it, God will not get the money, but you will not be able to keep it either. Somehow you will lose it." That very Sunday afternoon, lightning struck his two best horses, for which he had recently paid exactly $400, and killed them. He publicly blamed me for getting his horses killed.

When is wife told me to bring the whole church with me, I could not get them all, but I rounded up about four hundred people. We filled every nook and cranny of that large farm house. The front and back porches were filled, and the yard was loaded with people, crowding toward the house as best they could. It looked like a scene for the beginning of a great revival.

The wife asked, "Brother Ward, come and pray for my husband. He is upstairs in bed."

I answered, "No, I have a chair fixed in the living room. Tell him to come down and sit in this chair. God is going to heal him."

She replied, "You don't understand; he is dying; he can't get out of bed"

"God will give him strength to get out of bed," I cried. I was very young then, nineteen years old, you understand, and very hard-boiled, I guess, for a youngster. I would not be so cruel now.

At any rate, pretty soon I saw the deacon coming down the stairs in his bathrobe and slippers, and a little skullcap that farmers wore to bed in those days. He sat in the living room. He declared, "Before Brother Ward prays for me, I want to make a confession. I want to ask him and the whole church to forgive me."

I asked his wife if she had any oil. She replied that she only had a quart bottle of olive oil. I said, "Bring it on."

After he asked the whole church to forgive him, I got so happy I forgot what I was doing. I took off his skullcap. He was completely bald. Not fully realizing what I was doing, I turned that quart bottle of olive oil upside down over his head and began to rub the oil into his bald head.

The oil flowed down over his shoulders and all over him. He came out of that chair shouting, jumping to his feet. He gave a kick, and one of his slippers hit the ceiling. He gave another kick, and another slipper hit the ceiling. He began to dance in the spirit. He danced in and out of one room after another. He kept shouting, "I am healed! I am healed!"

He came back to church the next service and was the very best deacon that I ever had anywhere. A couple of months later, he told me, "Brother Ward, there is something that I have meant to tell you. Do you know that when you prayed for me and anointed me with oil, it seemed to me that I could feel that oil flowing all over me."

I answered, "Brother, if there is anything that I am absolutely certain about, it is that you were well-oiled.

1. How does God feel about sin?

_____

_____

2. Why does God feel the way He does about sin?

_____

_____

3. What should you do if you sin?

_____

_____

4. Is there anyone that you should ask forgiveness from?

_____

_____

CHAPTER 5

YOUR ENEMIES

As a believer you're going to have these two major enemies: your flesh and the devil. Most of the shots fired by either one of these enemies come in the form of thoughts to your mind. You may think that all of the thoughts in your mind come from you and you feel badly that you could think such things. No, temptations come to everyone in the form of thoughts and just because a certain thought pops into your mind does not mean you're guilty of that thought. You become guilty when you start to entertain the thought. If you immediately reject it, you have successfully resisted the temptation. However, if you begin to dwell on the thought, begin to consider taking some action resulting from the thought, then you become guilty.

One of the things NOT affected by the new birth is the flesh, the animal nature in humans that incites them to sin. Every cell of your flesh shouts "Don't believe the Bible! Don't believe the Bible!" Your flesh is the enemy of you, your spirit self.

I say then: Walk in the Spirit, and you shall not fulfill the lust of the flesh. For the flesh lusts against the Spirit, and the Spirit against the flesh; and these are contrary to one another, so that you do not do the things that you wish. But if you are led by the Spirit, you are not under the law. (Galatians 5:16-18)

As long as you live in your present physical body, your flesh is something that will not change. You will always have to be diligent in your stand against its influence. Reading further in Galatians we see the flesh and the spirit contrasted:

Now the works of the flesh are evident, which are: adultery, fornication, uncleanness, lewdness, idolatry, sorcery, hatred, contentions, jealousies, outbursts of wrath, selfish ambitions, dissensions, heresies, envy, murders, drunkenness, revelries, and the like; of which I tell you beforehand, just as I also told you in time past, that those who practice such things will not inherit the kingdom of God. But the fruit of the Spirit is love, joy, peace, longsuffering, kindness, goodness, faithfulness, gentleness, self-control. Against such there is no law. And those who are Christ's have crucified the flesh with its passions and desires. If we live in the Spirit, let us also walk in the Spirit. (Galatians 5:19-25)

Many times the temptations from the flesh come in the form of impulses. Once I saw a clear illustration of this kind of impulse and the bad result that came. Many cars were lined up in two lanes, bumper to bumper, waiting for a train to clear the tracks that cut across the road. A young man on a crossroad wanted to cross the road but was blocked by the waiting cars. When what he thought was an opening in traffic appeared, he angrily floored the gas pedal. His tires squealed and he shot into the intersection, hitting a car that he didn't see coming. His impatience caused his car plus another car to be smashed up, and he probably got a traffic ticket too. The train caused a delay, but his impatience caused a much longer delay plus some added expenses.

The devil, your other main enemy, also brings thoughts to your mind. It's important to neither underestimate him nor overestimate him. What you need to know about him is that he is a liar. If you do not believe his lies, he has no advantage over you. However, if you let your mind dwell on the lies he tells you, you can start to feel the effect in your emotions. This is because your emotions are controlled by your thoughts. Think scary thoughts and you'll become afraid.

There is no lie that is outside of the realm of the kind of things he might tell you. Of course he will side with your flesh and emphasize whatever your flesh might tempt you with. For example, have you ever gotten really angry about something, and afterwards you think to yourself "Why was I *so* angry?" What happened was that your flesh reacted in anger, but the devil amplified that anger. He gave you a shove in that direction. Also, any thought that brings feelings that are opposite to the fruit of the spirit, come from the devil. Thoughts of discouragement, depression, hopelessness and so on, come from him. He has videos, so to speak, of all your mistakes. He'll play those videos for you while speaking condemning thoughts to your mind.

Knowing the difference between condemnation and correction will help keep you in victory. When God deals with you about a sin in your life, He will show you clearly what it is. He will communicate with you about it in a way that uplifts you and shows you the way out of the difficulties associated with that sin. God's correction, when you receive it and obey it, will leave you at peace. Condemnation on the other hand, brings with it hopelessness and discouragement. It tells you you're bad and now you have finally ruined things forever and there's no way out, no solution.

Thank God for His word. His word is truth. Our defense against lies is the truth. We don't have to fight the devil, Jesus already defeated him. We let the word of God do the work. We do like Jesus did when Satan tempted Him. We say "It is written…" Clearly, the more of God's word you know, the more successful you will be against the lies of your enemy.

Another line of defense is to maintain your joy and peace. Paul prayed:

> *Now may the God of hope fill you with all joy and peace in believing, that you may abound in hope by the power of the Holy Spirit.* (Romans 15:13)

Joy and peace are products of believing. It's a danger signal when these fruits are not in your life. In the case of a car engine, when the indicators show that the oil pressure is low or the water is hot, the life of the engine is threatened. So it is with us. If our joy or peace level is low, it's a life threatening situation. No joy and no peace are some of the first signs of steps away from God.

We stay at peace by keeping a clear conscience. We keep a clean conscience by doing what's right and repenting when we miss it. We maintain joy by rejoicing. In many, many places, the Bible commands us to rejoice in the Lord. To rejoice means to be joyful. It may be news to you that you're the one who determines whether or not you're joyful. While it is true that good things can happen that produce joy in us, real joy is the joy you maintain regardless of circumstances. Real joy is constant because we rejoice in the Lord who never changes. Rejoice in the Lord by praising and thanking God. Tell Him why you love Him. Thank Him for what He's done for you. Thank Him for what you believe He will do for you.

1. What kind of enemies do you have?

   _____

   _____

2. What are your enemies' goals?

   _____

   _____

3. What are your weapons against your enemies?

   _____

   _____

4. What are your strategies for victory?

   _____

   _____

Conclusion

New Believer, I'm happy for you. I'm happy that you will remain with God forever. I'm glad that you're redeemed from destruction. I thank God that I was able to communicate these truths to you. I believe that you will find them as helpful to you as they have been to me. Have a great eternity!

What then shall we say to these things? If God is for us, who can be against us? He who did not spare His own Son, but delivered Him up for us all, how shall He not with Him also freely give us all things? Who shall bring a charge against God's elect? It is God who justifies. Who is he who condemns? It is Christ who died, and furthermore is also risen, who is even at the right hand of God, who also makes intercession for us. Who shall separate us from the love of Christ? Shall tribulation, or distress, or persecution, or famine, or nakedness, or peril, or sword? As it is written: "For Your sake we are killed all day long; We are accounted as sheep for the slaughter." Yet in all these things we are more than conquerors through Him who loved us. For I am persuaded that neither death nor life, nor angels nor principalities nor powers, nor things present nor things to come, nor height nor depth, nor any other created thing, shall be able to separate us from the love of God which is in Christ Jesus our Lord. (Romans 8:31-39)

If this book was helpful, you could help others find it by leaving a positive review on Amazon.

RECOMMENDED READS

Know Your Bible, Paul Kent and George Knight

7 Spiritual Habits That Can Change Your Life, Joey Clifton

How to Study the Bible (VALUE BOOKS), Robert M. West

The New Birth, Kenneth E. Hagin

.

About the Author

Thomas A. Lenz's life experience includes work as a jeweler, hang glider maker, mechanical engineer, professional musician, software developer, Bible school teacher and missionary. He is a member of RHEMA Ministerial Association International and holds a Bachelor of Science degree in Mechanical Engineering and a Masters of Theology degree. For most of the last twenty years he's served as a missionary as part of Jarva County Christian Center in Estonia. He currently lives in Estonia with his wife Beth, and sons Jed and Rock.

www.ingramcontent.com/pod-product-compliance
Lightning Source LLC
Chambersburg PA
CBHW080939040426
42443CB00015B/3477